Child Magical

a memoir

CECILE RAVELL

This is a Warrior Woman book

brought to you by Warrior Woman Press
https://ravellc.wixsite.com/ravell-the-writer

Copyright © Cecile Ravell 2021

The moral right of the author has been asserted in accordance with the Copyright Amendment (Moral Rights) Act 2000.
All rights reserved. Except as permitted under the Australian Copyright Act 1968 (for example, fair dealing for the purposes of study, research, criticism or review) no part of this publication may be reproduced, stored in a retrieval system, or transmitted in any form or by any means, electronic, mechanical, photocopying, recording or otherwise, without the written permission of the publisher.

Cataloguing-in-Publication entry is available from the National Library of Australia: http://catalogue.nla.gov.au/

Title: Child Magical
Author: Ravell, Cecile
ISBNs: 978-0-6450452-0-8 (paperback)
978-0-6450452-1-5 (ebook – epub)
Subjects: Biography and Autobiography/Personal Memoirs;
History/Australia and New Zealand;
Social Science/Emigration and Immigration

Names, events and character occupations have been changed to protect the privacy of individuals. The author has made every effort to ensure that the information in this book was correct at the time of publication. However, the author and publisher accept no liability for any loss, damage or disruption incurred by the reader or any other person arising from any action taken or not taken based on the content of this book. The author recommends seeking third party advice and considering all options prior to making any decision or taking action in regard to the content of this book.

Cover image: Shutterstock
Cover design: newartworx.com.au

This book is dedicated to the child magical in all of us, who has the gift of imagination, shows resilience in challenging circumstances, and sees life as an adventure.

Contents

One: A Journey	1
Babes In Brooklyn	3
Going To Multa	11
Flight To A Stralya	17
Two: A Place	23
Melrose Street	25
Flemington Road	33
Wedding Court	49
Three: An Era	61
All About Family	63
The Way Things Were	77
The Getting Of Wisdom	89
Acknowledgements	99
About the Author	100

One

A Journey

BABES IN BROOKLYN

Humble Beginnings

'Quick, sis, quick! Come outside.'

I left my doll on the sofa and ran to the window. My hero was calling me from the pavement below.

'Coming, Fwanken.' My three-year-old tongue struggled to pronounce 'Franklyn'.

'Hurry up,' my brother urged as I tottered down the front steps.

He grabbed my hand and took off at a trot, dragging me behind him. We rounded the corner of the last house on The Block and Franklyn pointed downwards.

'He's in here. Quick!'

I drew back from the dankness of the room.

Oh, no, not another basement!

A chunky kid glared up at me through his sweat-matted red fringe.

'Go on, sis, bite him.'

Roly-poly cringed. Obviously, my reputation had preceded me.

'Okay, Fwanken.'

We moved forward and the boy took off, scurrying like a rat towards the internal staircase. In his haste, he stumbled. We were on him in a flash – Franklyn holding him while I bit into his taut flesh. The boy yelped, then started to cry.

No, don't cry.

I backed off – I got upset when kids cried. After all, it was just a friendly bite. That's what the Maltese did to show affection, didn't they? I was confused.

'Bite him again.'

'No, Fwanken. Let him go.'

The boy scrambled up the steps, making his escape.

Franklyn put his arm around my shoulder. 'Good job, sis. He won't try stealing my marbles again.'

That evening, there was a loud knock at the door.

'Missus, I've come to talk to you about your children. They ganged up on my poor Budd.'

We poked our heads around the corner of the door and looked up at the massive form of Roly-poly's mom.

Eek!

Mrs Roly-poly looked down at our cherubic

faces. How could these two angels have dispatched her huge son in such a brutal way?

'S-sorry, my mistake, missus. He must have got the wrong address.' Mrs Roly-poly left shaking her head.

'Franklyn!' Mom was mad. 'What have you been up to?'

'He's a bully – he twisted my arm and stole my marbles. And … and … he is bigger than me. I needed help,' Franklyn said in his defence.

'Wait until your father gets home.'

As usual, Franklyn was spared the threatened punishment; he had a way of twisting our father around his little finger. A technique I never learned – Mom said I wasn't born with Franklyn's 'rat-cunning'.

Back to the Basement

'Okay, sweetheart, off to bed.'

'But, Mommy, it's early. Why is Fwanken still up?'

'He's older. You can stay up late when you're his age.'

Mom took my hand and led me down the winding staircase into the basement. *Urgh!* I hated the basement. The walls vibrated because there were monsters inside them, waiting to creep out and gobble me up in the middle of the night.

My crib was in a small alcove where I slept with my life-sized doll Susie. She came in handy whenever my chewing-gum bubble burst when Mom was still within earshot.

'Did I hear you blowing bubbles?' my mother would say, raising an eyebrow.

'It was Susie.' I would quickly thrust the gum into her mouth. Of course, my mother believed me. I thought I was so clever learning how to lie from observing my older brother.

'Say your prayers now.'

I prayed every night, because I knew God would protect me from the monsters – that's his job, you know.

'Now I name me down to sleep, I pray the Lord my soul to sheep. If I should die before I wait, I pray the Lord my sole to take.' Oh, well, that's what it sounded like to me. I never could figure out why the Lord wanted the soles of my shoes after I was dead. And I didn't understand why Mom always left with a big smile on her face.

I Wouldn't Be Caught Dead in That!

I pressed my nose to the frosty window, watching Franklyn throwing snowballs at the other kids from The Block. I had woken up with a slight temperature and Daddy said I was confined to quarters. He'd been a company sergeant major in the army, and when he gave an order, it was to be obeyed.

After agonising for fifteen minutes, watching the

kids outside, I pleaded with Mom. 'I want to play with Fwanken.'

'No, sweetheart, you can't go out. You're sick.'

'I want to play with Fwanken. Please, pleeeeease.'

'You'll get pneumonia.'

'Please,' I whimpered.

'Okay, okay! But only if you dress up in something warm.'

'Anything, anything.'

Little did I know that this promise would come back to haunt me. In her desire to protect me from the bitter cold, my mother – in all her wisdom – decided my brother's concert clown outfit, worn *over* my snowsuit, would shield me from the harsh elements.

'I don't want to wear the clown suit,' I screeched.

'It will keep you warm. Remember, you must take care of your singing voice. You're not going out unless you wear it.'

I stamped my foot and offered my chubby arm to be draped in the hideous suit. I perched my 'Muggsy' hat on my head so I wouldn't look completely ridiculous.

If only parents knew how their well-seeming actions can scar their children for life. In fact, the reason I didn't become a ballerina can be traced back to the clown suit. But that's another story.

Early Rebellion

'Say "excuse me", young lady!' Daddy had his 'serious' face on.

'No!' I'd burped out loud, and it made Franklyn giggle.

'You'd better apologise, because I don't want anyone with bad manners living in my house.'

'No!' I don't know why I refused to apologise – maybe I was going through a phase, or maybe it was because every time I said 'no', Franklyn burst into a fit of laughter.

'Well, I think you'd better go pack your bag, young lady, and leave.'

'Are you coming, Fwanken?'

'No way! It's dark and cold out there. And there's a big dog at the end of the lane.'

So much for brotherly love! And to think I'd worn a hideous clown suit to play with him.

''Scuse me,' I said in my most coquettish voice. 'May I have dessert now?'

Daddy was pretending to scowl, but I knew he'd been kidding. Well, at least, I hope so!

You Should be on the Stage, Sis.

'Ladies and gentlemen, presenting the Darling of Brooklyn, with her endishen of 'Pennies from Heaven'.' Franklyn hammed it up as the Master of Ceremonies.

I emerged from behind the heavy crimson drapes in our parlour to the tumultuous applause of Mommy, Daddy, Auntie, Jimmy, and my godparents. This was the last time I would see my godparents before we set sail for 'Multa', so I was treating them to one of my exclusive performances.

'Every time it rains it rains pennies from heaven.' I twirled my pink parasol, which matched my ballerina dress and sheer gloves – Mommy was such a stickler for dressing me 'a la mode'. I flicked my Shirley Temple ringlets that Auntie had spent all day curling – but mine were black, not blond. *Sigh*.

'Don't you know each cloud contains …' Daddy loved to teach me songs and I loved to sing – I added my own choreography.

When I sang the part about finding your fortune falling all over town, I turned my parasol upside down and took a little jump back. It brought a round of applause from my adoring fans.

'Save them for a package of … sunshine and flowers.' I moved my hand around in an arc to show where these would come from – in case my audience wasn't sure.

'If you want the things you love … you must have showers.' This seemed a good philosophy and it started me along a path of optimism.

I belted out the last line of the song, 'There'll be pennies from heaven for you and me,' and disappeared behind the drapes to the thunderous applause and calls for an encore.

Years later, Mommy told me a talent scout had offered to put me on the stage. My parents felt Franklyn would feel left out if they'd agreed. Their decision denied me a career in show biz, but I was destined to be on the stage – in one way or another!

GOING TO MULTA

The Voyage

The ship rolled from side to side. We were feeling sick, so Franklyn and I went on deck to get some fresh air. As we leaned against each other for support from the blustering wind, we were approached by one of the stewards. Bruno, who'd taken a shine to us, gently cupped my face in one of his large calloused hands, hugging Franklyn towards him with the other.

'*Bambini*, whatsa da mat?' He talked funny – like Chico Marx.

'Why won't this ship stop rocking?' I wailed.

'*Poverini*,' he cooed, with kindness in his grey eyes.

We were going to a country called 'Multa'. Mommy, Daddy, and Auntie were born there, and it's where most of their family lived. We were going all that way because Auntie and Jimmy wanted to have their wedding there. Getting married must be worth it, I thought, because we were all risking *death by vomiting* to get there!

Finally, we docked at a place called 'Kyrow'. It was so hot I thought I would melt like the Wicked Witch of the West. When we got off the boat, we were surrounded by a mob of people trying to sell us all sorts of stuff. To prevent us from being crushed to death, and stave off the hawkers, Mommy bought me a beautiful camel leather pocketbook. I loved the way a scene of the pyramids and palm trees had been painted in red, orange, and green. I didn't have it for long – my mother made me give it to my 'kuzin' Natalie, because she was a 'Miss Keena'. (I later found out *miskina* means 'poor thing' in Maltese – like *poverina* in Italian). It started a life-long pattern of Mom convincing me to give away much-loved possessions.

After a long journey, we got to Malta – I learned how to spell it when writing to my Aunt Kitty – another *miskina*. There sure were a lot of them in Malta!

I discovered I had lots of kuzins when we were swamped at the docks. I nearly got smothered with all the kissing and hugging. Mom said they were just glad to see us. Apparently, that's how you express affection in Malta – by suffocating people!

We piled into a couple of taxis and were taken to Uncle John's house. He was a famous opera singer.

After we ate enough food to sustain a small African nation, we got to hear him sing. It was okay, but I didn't understand the words, and it didn't hold a candle to 'Pennies from Heaven'.

I met my grandma for the first time – the only grandparent I still had living. She was scary – all dressed in black with long, grey, plaited hair rolled in a bun. When she uncoiled it at night, it looked like a giant snake slithering down her back. *Eek!*

She was grumpy about everything, especially cats who tried to eat her 'pet' pigeons. I found out later that it was because she wanted to eat them herself.

What a horrible person!

It Doesn't Rain…

Malta is a tiny island – even smaller than Brooklyn! Mom told us it was always hot and sunny; it had beaches and sand and everything. We were supposed to go swimming every day; alas, parents will say anything to get you on a boat!

It had started to rain the day after we arrived and didn't stop for three months, or so it seemed. Stuck indoors, we played with our newly discovered cousins. Yep, I learned how to spell that too!

'Look, Natalie. *Imsielet.*' (The Maltese word for earrings.) I hung the double stalk of plump cherries on her ear and she clapped her hands. She was easy to entertain. Natalie was half my age – only two. I thought that's why she was a bit vague, until I overheard her mom saying she was 'slow'. I didn't care how fast she was – I liked her! She was my substitute doll; I had to leave Susie behind in Brooklyn because she was too big to pack in a case. I really missed her.

I was distracted from my daydreaming by Franklyn, yelling and laughing because he'd won some marbles from our boy cousins. I gazed at the boys playing and dreamed of the day I would have my own bag of cats' eyes.

'Please, Fwanken, can I play?' My four-year-old tongue still got tangled on his name.

'Okay, sis, but you have to give me half of what you win.'

What a 'horse trader', as Daddy used to say.

The other boys gawked in amazement as Franklyn handed over six cats' eyes and welcomed me into the circle. My cousins complained that girls weren't supposed to do 'boy stuff', but they let me play because they saw a chance to win their marbles back.

I cleaned up that day and was able to repay Franklyn, with interest. The cousins eyed us with suspicion and, from then on, we were known as the 'hustlers from America'.

The Wedding

We spent the whole of the next week preparing for the wedding and, finally, the big day came.

Franklyn was all dressed up in a black suit, white shirt, and white bow tie. My big brother really looked like the Master of Ceremonies.

Auntie was a different story – she looked like a meringue! Whoever told her that short, round people could wear fluffy, full-length dresses really 'sold her a bill of goods', as Daddy said. Her chubby face was the picture of joy, and I was happy she didn't know how funny she looked.

A big, black limousine pulled up and Franklyn climbed into the back with Auntie and the flower girl.

'See you later, sis!'

The car pulled away and I could see him grinning back at me through the rear window. I felt sad; because I wasn't in the wedding party I didn't get to ride with them. My parents' budget didn't run to two outfits, so Franklyn was the 'chosen one'. He was gloating, as usual.

'Come along, sweetheart. We're going with Uncle John.'

What a consolation prize! Uncle John was a worrywart. He reminded me of a kettle boiling because he was always agitated; I swear I could see steam coming out of his ears.

'Hurry up! Hurry up!' he thundered.

Boy, no wonder he could sing opera – his speaking voice could shatter glass! Despite his panic attack, we got to the church in plenty of time.

Franklyn walked down the aisle on his own, proud as punch. When he got to the altar, he handed the satin cushion to the altar boy and dashed back to our pew. In a high pitch, he started chanting, 'Dum … dum, da-dum … dum, da-dum, da-dum, da-dum.'

'Franklyn!' Mom looked flustered. 'Stop that. It's the 'Funeral March'!'

Franklyn had that impish grin on his face, which always made Daddy laugh, so of course he'd get away with it – *again*.

The people around us looked mortified and my mother's face turned bright red. Thank goodness the organist started playing the 'Wedding March' and all heads turned to watch the meringue float down the aisle.

Jimmy was waiting at the altar, his face bursting with love as he watched Auntie coming towards him. Her eldest brother, Frederick, was 'giving her away' because her father was no longer alive.

A week later, Uncle Frederick died of a stroke and everyone eyed Franklyn with dread.

We'd come to Malta for a wedding and got a funeral as a bonus. We left for 'A stralya' with the reputation of being 'hustlers' and the stigma of killing our uncle!

FLIGHT TO A STRALYA

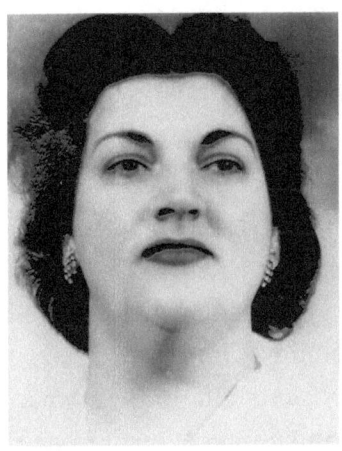

A Baby Kangaroo

I was lost in a forest of legs as the big people clung to each other, hugging and sobbing.

Hey ... look out!

No one had died, not since Franklyn jinxed Uncle Frederick. I couldn't figure out why everyone was so sad.

Mommy had been sick for a few months, then started to get a big tummy – she was turning into a roly-poly. Daddy seemed to think it would cheer her up if we got her a baby kangaroo, and you could only get them in 'A stralya'. So, there we were at the airport, waiting for our flight. Once again, we were crushed by all our Maltese family. They were hugging us and weeping.

After we peeled ourselves away from their clutching arms, we walked across a big road called 'the runway'. Mommy and Daddy kept looking back and waving. Franklyn and I just wanted to get out of there.

We clambered up a long flight of stairs leading to the big silver tube of the plane. When we got inside, there were lots of people fidgeting in their seats or storing their luggage into shelves above. Most of them looked sad, but a few of them were happy and excited, like me and my brother.

We found our seats and Mommy clipped my belt around my tummy. Of course, Franklyn couldn't sit still. Daddy spoke to him in his *big* voice and Franklyn stopped squirming long enough to be belted into his seat.

A voice spoke, from somewhere, welcoming us to the flight and telling us to keep our seat belts on at all times.

There was a lull from the passengers' chatting, as the plane's engines roared. It started to move, then got *really* fast. I felt like I was floating, and when I looked out the window, that's what we were doing. I thought we were being lifted to heaven by God's invisible fingers.

Oh! Calcutta

'Sweetheart, wake up! Look at the beautiful sunrise.' Mom was shaking my arm.

I peeked out the window through bleary eyes. A big orange ball was melting the black sky. 'Wow!'

'Would you like some breakfast, little lady?' The stewardess placed a tray with cornflakes and juice on a table that popped out from the seat in front.

Magic!

After breakfast, the voice said we would be landing in Calcutta soon. Mommy wiped our faces with the warm washcloth the stewardess gave her, then tried to comb the tangles out of my hair. *Ouch! That hurts!* Curly, smurly – I wished my hair was straight.

Franklyn had escaped his belt and was running up and down the aisle. The voice spoke again, telling us to fasten our seat belts. The passengers looked relieved when Daddy snatched up Franklyn – *the pest* – and strapped him in.

The plane felt like it was bumping down steps. There was a big 'whoosh' as it hit the ground, and we were all thrown back in our seats. The fast plane became slower and started following a brown man who was on the ground waving a couple of coloured table tennis bats.

'Ladies and gentlemen, please remain in your seats until the aircraft is disinfected.'

When the plane stopped, some more brown people in uniforms got on and sprayed the cabin.

'Why are they spraying, Mommy?' I was always asking 'why'.

'They're making sure there are no insects, sweetheart.'

Yuk! I looked around my seat to see if I'd sat on any.

We were allowed to stand up and everyone grabbed at their luggage. They pressed forward against the passengers in front of them to make them move faster. I was trapped in the legs, *again*, and my Muggsy hat fell off. Daddy elbowed a couple of passengers out of the way and scooped me up in his arms. When we got to the door, a hot blast of air hit me in the face. I could hardly breathe.

Oh! Calcutta was not going to be a nice place.

One More Sleep

The heat was rising off the pavement as we walked back from the restaurant. Mom had bought us a bag of marshmallows, and a swarm of grubby children in tatty clothes were following us with their hands outstretched.

'Poor things,' Mom said. 'Drop the bag and keep walking, sweetheart.'

Not again. It seemed like the world was full of people who we needed to pity – I'd been *so* enjoying eating my marshmallows.

I couldn't wait to get away from that place. Thank goodness we had an early flight out the next day.

The plane landed in Darwin at night and we got out to stretch our legs. Franklyn ran off with some boys and Mom and I went shopping. *Yay!*

'Come on, let's get something for your birthday, sweetheart,' Mom said.

I chose a cute brooch with little glass fruit hanging from it, hoping I would not meet another Miss Keena and have to give it away! At that moment, one of the boys came running up to Mommy.

'He's bleeding all over the place.'

Yes, it was Franklyn, *again!* He'd jumped over a fence and there were panes of glass resting on the other side. You guessed it – of all the boys, he's the one who crashed onto the glass, a shard piercing his ankle.

Mommy and Daddy had to frantically look for a doctor. That was the end of my birthday shopping. *Pest!*

All stitched up and bandaged, Franklyn was 'milking it for all it was worth', Daddy said, carrying him onto the plane. The passengers pretended to pity him, but I bet they were glad he couldn't run up and down the aisle – they probably put a curse on him. People do that, you know.

Unexpectedly, all the passengers began singing *Happy Birthday*. This time, I was the special one.

I was five now and I could go to school – just like Franklyn.

Two

A Place

MELROSE STREET

Room at the top

I crept into our upstairs room in my Auntie Mary's house in case my mother was asleep with the baby. The room was dark, but I could see her sitting at the only window facing Melrose Street. She looked like a beautiful, framed painting, half in shade and half in light.

As I ran up to her, she turned, and I saw tears in her eyes. I leaned against her knee, then reached up and patted her face.

'Hello, sweetheart. Why aren't you outside playing?' She smiled, pretending she hadn't been crying.

'It's so hot, Mummy.' That's what children called their mothers here. 'The black stuff on the footpath is melting and my shoes are getting stuck. Look!'

'Quick, take them off. I don't want to give *him* another reason to complain.'

The 'him' she was talking about was my Auntie's husband. I had heard my mum and dad whispering late at night that he'd made it clear we had 'outstayed our welcome' – whatever that meant.

'Why are you always sad now, Mummy?'

She'd been unhappy since coming home from the hospital. If someone gave me a baby instead of a kangaroo, I'd be sad too, especially after travelling all the way from Malta.

'I miss my sister Doris, and my friends in New York. I miss having our own apartment.'

I did too. But most of all I missed my doll Susie.

'When are we going home, Mummy?'

'Soon, sweetheart. I'm going to get a job at the place where Auntie Mary works, and when I save enough money, we can go back.'

I said, 'Yay,' clapped my hands, spun like a top until I got dizzy, and collapsed on the rug. I struggled to my feet.

Mum held out her arms for me to get a cuddle. 'You *will* look after the baby when I'm at work, won't you?'

The baby, Lenny, was almost as big as Susie. My mum said it was because she was 'pre-di-bettic' when he was born.

'He's so heavy and I'm only little.'

'It's just until Daddy gets home from work. You'll only have to watch him to make sure he doesn't roll off the bed. Anyway, I'm not going to start working until we move out of here.'

'Where will we go?' I frowned because we didn't know anyone else in Australia – yep, that's how you spell it!

'Daddy has found us a nice bungalow behind a milk bar. We'll be moving before you start school.'

All I could think of at that moment was the lolly counter – with freckles and buddies and other yummy stuff. Then I realised Mum had said 'school'.

'Can we go buy my uniform now, Mummy? Can we? Can we?'

'We can't take the baby out in this heat. We'll go tomorrow if it's cooler. Now go outside and play.'

The Games People Play

Melrose Street had a raised strip in the middle, covered in grass. It was green despite the scorching summer sun, because 'the fairies come out at night and sprinkle it with water', Franklyn had said. I tried to stay up late each night to see them, but always fell asleep. By the morning, they'd gone.

My cousins were playing a game called British Bulldog with some other big kids.

'Can I play, please?'

'Okay, squirt. These are the rules: you have to try and run past us and reach the goal post.' My cousin George pointed to the strip sign that said: 'keep left'.

I took off as fast as I could. My much older cousin 'Big Louey' grabbed me, turned me upside down, dropped me to the ground, and yelled, 'British Bulldog.'

Our older boy cousins always played games in which Franklyn and I ended up getting injured. Whenever they weren't throwing us about, they were scaring us out of our wits with ghost stories. They weren't very nice people, treating us as though we were a nuisance – like their father did.

'I don't want to play this game anymore,' I said, rubbing my grazed elbow.

Off I went to look for Franklyn. I found him down the lane with the 'rough' kid from the metal-recycling yard.

'Can I play with you, Franklyn? Please, please.'

'Okay, but don't get in our way. We're looking for treasure. And don't tell Mum.'

I didn't know what they thought they'd find in the pile of junk, but I went along just the same.

The lanes were forbidden territory and we weren't supposed to play with the 'rough' kids. Yes, they swore a lot, wore dirty clothes, and didn't wear shoes, but they never dropped us from a great height or teased us, as our cousins did.

We got to their lane and went into the yard. The metal was piled a million feet high. The sun flashed off the surfaces, making it look like a magic mountain.

Franklyn climbed up one side; the 'rough' kid, Jimmy, climbed up the other side. The aim was to find the treasure first. At that moment, I heard a woman's voice shouting, 'What da youse kids think you're doin'? Get down off there before I come out and frottle ya.'

I hid behind the fence, trembling in my shoes. Franklyn and Jimmy scrambled down – and wouldn't you know it, Franklyn cut himself on a piece of metal.

I burst into tears because I knew we would both cop it from Dad when we got home.

'Don't worry, sis, it's just a scratch.'

I wasn't having any of it. We were going to get a hiding, for sure. *And* with the leather strap.

Jimmy's mum – she wasn't scary after all – came out with Dettol, cleaned up the wound, and put a Band-Aid on Franklyn's hand.

'Now off with youse and don't let me catch ya on the pile again, or I'll box yer ears. Jimmy, get yaself inside.'

Franklyn took my hand and I stopped crying. We raced down the lane, back into Melrose Street. The sun was setting and Dad would be home soon.

We sneaked in the front door and tiptoed up the stairs to our room where Mum was sleeping on the big bed with Lenny. We lay down next to them and pretended to be asleep.

Dad walked into the room and found his two angels snuggled up. He came over and kissed us. I held my breath; when he didn't notice Franklyn's Band-Aid, I let it out with a big sigh.

'What's that sigh all about, Muggsy?' My dad used

the nickname he gave me back in Brooklyn; Muggsy was a kid in a TV program I loved to watch.

'I'm just glad to see you, Daddy. Did you have a good day at work?' *Phew, that was a close one.*

'Yes, I did, sweetheart. Thank you. Look what I brought home.' He produced two Fry's chocolate cream bars; after pay-day, he always brought home candy.

'Don't tell Mum. You can have them after dinner. Have you washed your hands?'

We squirmed out from under Mum's arm and raced to see who could get to the bathroom first. My brother won and grinned at me like he was the king of the castle.

Mr Car-waana's Picture Night

My Auntie Mary had cooked rabbit stew – she called it *stuffata* – and served it up with spaghetti sauce with hard peas in it. I pushed it around a while until it looked like the pile was getting smaller. *How could people eat bunny rabbits?* She was as bad as my grandmother who ate her pigeons.

After dinner, our cousins said they were going to Mr Car-waana's to watch the 'flicks'.

'May we go, Daddy? Please, sir, we ate all our vegg-ables.' Franklyn knew when to use his best manners to get his way.

'Okay, but stay with your cousins. Make sure you walk home with them afterwards.'

We scrambled off our chairs and headed for the door. When we got outside, our cousins tore off down Melrose Street, leaving us behind.

'Don't worry, sis, we'll ride our horses.'

We climbed on our pretend mounts and galloped down the street.

'Come on, Shadow, giddy up,' Franklyn said to his horse. He always got the black one. I got the boring white one, so I imagined it was a unicorn.

We raced the length of Melrose Street, around the corner, and up the hill to get to the Car-waanas. In contrast to my Auntie's ugly red-brick, concrete-paved prison, their house was made of wood, painted white, with a blue lace fringe of wrought iron along the veranda. There was a wicker chair rocking in the evening breeze and a garden with all sorts of flowers. As we walked up the front steps, I stopped to run my hands through the lavender, releasing a lovely fragrance from its lilac petals.

'Come on, sis, we'll be late for the *pastizzi*.'

When Mrs Car-waana opened the door, the smell hit us. *Yum*. Even though my auntie's kitchen always smelled of *pastizzi*, we weren't allowed to have any; her husband made and sold them for a living.

'Ay-ya, Ay-ya,' Mrs Car-waana said. It meant 'come on, come on' in Maltese. She waddled ahead, urging us to follow. 'Dee udders are here already. Dee picture she is starting.' She had a funny way of talking, but we knew what she meant.

'Sit down, we start picture now,' said Mr

Car-waana, the other half of the 'roly-poly' couple.

He switched off the lights, and the movie reel started on the projector. Scary music sounded, then the title appeared: *Doctor X*.

Oh, no. That didn't sound good.

The picture was about a man who got 'lectrocuted'. He didn't die; he just ended up with a white streak in his hair. It left him in a bad mood, so he went around killing people. I would never again be able to watch a movie with Humphrey Bogart in it without remembering *Doctor X*.

I kept my eyes shut most of the time, but I could still hear the screams. When it was over, we walked home in front of our cousins; they kept creeping up behind us, grabbing us by the shoulders, and shouting, 'Boo!'

Boy, was I glad we wouldn't be living with them for much longer.

FLEMINGTON ROAD

Mrs Lola's Bungalow

Two weeks before the school year started, we moved to Mrs Lola's. Her bungalow was in the backyard of the milk bar. We weren't allowed to go through the shop to get to it; instead, we had to walk down the broken side-path. We risked twisting our ankles or, worse still, being bitten by a snake. They hide in the long grass, ya know.

Mr Lola was as tall as a gum tree. He had grey hair and wore a tatty beige 'cardie' most of the time. He used to shuffle about outside our bungalow, pretending to weed the garden. He'd wave and wink at my brother and me when he saw us staring out the window.

Mrs Lola looked like a dried-up tree branch, one that would crumble in a strong wind. Unlike her friendly husband, she never smiled or said hello and she used to shush us when we ran around the garden playing.

Mum didn't want any trouble, so we stayed indoors thinking up new games. One day, my mother was out shopping, and Dad was doing his crossword. Franklyn whispered, 'Hey, sis, put your finger in here.'

The 'here' was the socket of a lamp that was part of a radio. Ever the trusting sister, I stuck in my finger. Unbeknown to me, my brother had turned on the radio. I got a shock. Franklyn held his sides laughing while I looked at my finger, trying to work out why it was tingling. I never played that game again.

My First Day at School

At last, it was February and I was starting school. When she'd got her first paycheque, Mum had taken me down the street to buy my uniform. I couldn't wait to go to St Michael's. I was so excited the night before, I kept waking Franklyn to ask, 'Is it time to get up?'

'Go to sleep, weirdo.'

I couldn't work out why he didn't share my enthusiasm for school.

Mum brushed my hair and put it in plaits – that was school 'rega-lations' – tying them with green ribbons at the ends.

When we got out onto Flemington Road, Mum took my hand. 'Come on, sweetheart. Hold onto the pram. Franklyn! Stop running. Get back here.'

My brother couldn't behave, even on our first day of school. *Pest!*

Mum bent forward, pushing the pram with the lump of my baby brother inside. It was a long way, and I was growing tired. I wished I could get a ride like Lenny did.

We got to a huge red-brick building and walked through a tiny opening to the cemented grounds inside. I looked up at the wall; Jesus was hanging from a cross, larger than life. *Poor Jesus.*

There were heaps of kids talking in small groups. Some were running around – boys, of course. Franklyn took off after them. So much for looking after his little sister.

'Sweetheart, stand here against the wall in the shade until the bell goes.' Mum bent down to give me a cuddle and a kiss. 'Here's a cookie to eat at playtime. After I cash Dad's paycheque, I'll bring you money to buy lunch at the tuck-shop. Meet me at this spot. Okay?'

When she was gone, I stood with my arms crossed over my chest to comfort myself with the memory of her hug. At that moment, a boy ran up and kissed me on the cheek.

'You're beautiful,' he said. He pressed something into my hand, then ran away. To my surprise, it was a Mickey Mouse sharpener – not a bad exchange for a kiss.

All the bubs (first year kids) were gathered up by a rickety old nun wearing a saggy brown dress and a headscarf. I wondered if she was bald until I saw a whole bunch of nuns dressed the same.

The old nun steered the bubs grade kids along a corridor to an enormous room. The sun coming through the tall windows lit up the dust floating in the air. I thought I was going to choke on the musty smell.

'Choose a seat and a partner to sit with.' The nun pointed to lots of desks lined up in neat rows. I ran to the back seat of the end row – I wanted to be as far away from her as possible. A sweet girl with dark hair like mine sat next to me. Her name was Angelina. She was from Italy.

'Now stand up, children. We're going to recite the Lord's Prayer.' The old nun lifted both her hands in case we didn't know which way was up.

All the kids bowed their heads. Some of them closed their eyes and brought their palms together, raising them to their chests. They started praying and I could hear that a lot of them didn't know the words. I did, because my dad said the Rosary with us every night.

After prayers, the nun made us line up at the front of the room and picked out a girl from the group. Her name was Julie. She had pink skin, blue eyes, and golden hair in ringlets; she looked like Shirley Temple.

'Now, children, I want you to look at Julie because this is what an angel looks like.

Angelina and I turned to each other. I'm sure we were thinking the same thing: *So, what are we? Sinners!*

The first lesson was the alphabet. It was already written at the top of the board along with pictures of words that started with each letter – 'big A, little a, a for apple', we repeated in chorus. 'Big B, little b, b for boat …'

After the alphabet, the bell rang for playtime. *Yay!* I couldn't wait to get out in the sunshine and dust-free air – then I saw the crate of tiny milk bottles. *Oh no!*

'Now, everyone, take a bottle and drink it all up. Don't leave any – there are children starving in Africa, you know. Always remember you are fortunate to live in Australia and to come to a Catholic school.' Our old nun looked straight at me and Angelina.

I hated plain milk; I don't know why, I just could not drink it. When our nun wasn't looking, I sneaked away and went searching for Franklyn. I found him skylarking with some boys from our neighbourhood.

'Here, Franklyn … drink my milk, please.'

He downed it in one gulp.

'Thanks, sis. See you at lunchtime.'

I hurried back to our class gathering. The kids were still drinking their milk. I put my bottle back in the crate, and the next thing I knew, I was dragged out in front of the group by the nun and strapped around the legs.

I let out a wail.

The nun hollered at me, 'I didn't tell you to put

your bottle back in the crate. Next time wait until you're told.' She turned to glare at the other kids, who were trembling in their shoes as they clung to their bottles.

Well, if anything was going to spoil your first day at school, that was right up there.

At lunchtime, I met Franklyn and we walked towards the gate to meet Mum and get our tuck-shop money.

When we got there, she was standing with the pram in the shade. Her face was red. I thought it was because of the heat until she said, 'Bloody nun. Told me to get out of the way. Expected me to stand in the sun with the baby. I told her a thing or two: "Who the hell do you think you are, talking to me that way? If you have a sacrament, so do I. What do you have to show for it? I have three children."'

I didn't dare show her the strap marks on my legs. She was 'loaded and hunting for bear', as Dad would say.

'Geez, Mum, that's tellin' her.' Franklyn giggled.

'Here's your lunch money. I'll see you before I go to work. If any of those nuns look sideways at you, let me know.' Mum's colour had returned to normal now that she'd let off steam.

Off we ran to buy a pie with sauce, a bottle of Coke, and a meringue with sprinkles. We sat on the concrete and wolfed down our steaming pie, burning our mouths in the process. The Coke was a welcome balm, and the sweetness of the meringue helped to wipe out the bitterness of the nun's punishment.

My first day at school didn't turn out to be as great as I thought. No wonder Franklyn hadn't been excited.

I Wanted to be a Ballerina

I settled into school after learning the ropes – how to not get the strap – and found there were some good things about it. We got a *John and Betty* book; it had lovely pictures but dumb stories. 'This is John, this is Betty.' I loved reading, spelling, and doing sums. Most of all, I loved gymnastics and ballet.

At the end of the year, we had a school concert. Some of the girls were chosen to dance a ballet. The girl selected to be the fairy queen got to wear a silver crown and carry a wand. I longed to be the fairy queen, but I was chosen to be one of the fairies. Mum made me a beautiful pink net dress and painted my black ballet slippers to match. She said I looked like a doll.

After seeing the concert, my mother was so impressed with my dancing that she decided to send me to ballet school. A Maltese friend of hers had a daughter who was already attending classes. She was older than me and picked me up on her way. After the first few lessons, I knew how to get there and went by myself.

We were practising for a mid-year ballet-school concert when the teacher asked if anyone could do acrobatics. A couple of us put up our hands. *Big mistake*. I was chosen to play Puck in a scene from *Midsummer Night's Dream*. And just in case the audience didn't realise Puck was a prankster, I was to wear a clown suit. *No way*.

The memory of being dressed in a clown suit to go out in the Brooklyn snow made me cringe all over again. My mother had added the suit on top of several layers of clothing to protect me from catching a cold. I felt my cheeks burn, thinking of how the other kids had laughed at me, and I was determined to do whatever it took to avoid being embarrassed again.

The next Saturday, instead of going to the ballet lesson, I went on a little adventure. I caught the tram to Errol Street and went to the movies. The lesson money stretched to fish and chips, and an icy pole, if I didn't catch the tram back to Flemington Road.

It turned out I loved the movies more than ballet. I kept up my Saturday adventure until Mum's Maltese friend asked her if I was sick. Her daughter had squealed on me.

I was grounded; no more ballet, no more movies, and no more 'sweetheart'.

New Digs

When I was halfway through Grade One, we had to shift houses *again*. Mrs Lola said she was having a nervous breakdown because of the noise my brother and I were making inside the bungalow. *For goodness sake!*

We moved to a share-house about six doors up from the milk bar. The bedrooms at the front were rented by three young men who'd recently arrived from Malta. Charlie, Joey, and Andy were like good uncles.

Charlie – he pronounced it 'Chully' – looked after us between the time our mother left for night-shift until our father got home.

'You want pieces of toast and cups of tea?' He offered us refreshments every afternoon when we came home from school.

'Yes please,' Franklyn and I answered in unison. Franklyn didn't like tea, he just wanted to eat the Nestle condensed milk out of the can.

Yuk!

Franklyn and I got stuck into the toast. Lenny, who for some reason Charlie called 'Lillian', tottered towards the table. Seeing him struggling to get on a chair, Charlie helped him up. Such a kind man.

Apart from the new uncles, it was a great place to live because my brother and I got a bedroom separate from our parents. From the top bunk of our bed, we could look out a small window and see the sky. At night, we gazed at the stars, making up stories until our dad told us to go to sleep.

One night, Franklyn came up with a bright idea. 'Sis, I know a way we can get some extra sleep in the morning.'

I was game.

'Let's put on our uniforms and wear our pyjamas

on top. Then we can get out of bed later because we're already dressed.'

Dad came in to kiss us goodnight. 'What's this? Get out of bed. Take those clothes off and get back in your pyjamas. I'm going to get the belt.'

Oh no. I started crying.

Franklyn came to the rescue. 'Don't worry, sis. Shove these newspapers down the back of your pyjama pants. When Dad straps us, pretend it hurts and yell out.'

It seemed a good plan.

Dad walked in with the leather strap and was limbering up. 'You know the drill – bend over the chair. You first, Franklyn.'

My brother bent over, and I saw that the newspaper was sticking out. *Uh-oh,* so did Dad. I squeezed my eyes closed; I couldn't bear to look. Then something unexpected happened. Dad started chuckling. I took a peek. Yep, he was cracking up all right.

'Just get to bed, the two of you, and never let me catch you doing this again.' He walked off, shaking his head.

Phew. That was a close one.

I decided then and there I would not listen to any more of my brother's hair-brained ideas.

Cecile Ravell

More Holy than Righteous

'Stand still, sweetheart, so Guisa can pin the hem straight.'

I was trying on my First Holy Communion dress, swirling from side to side as I looked at myself in the mirror. The skirt was the fullest I'd ever had, and so pretty, with little embroidered holes in the material. The veil was net and made me look like a bride doll.

On Sunday, I was going to be married to Jesus. I couldn't wait.

The sunshine through the tiny window stirred me awake. I blinked, stretched, and turned towards the clock. *Oh no.* It was 8:30. I had to be at the church by 9:00.

I ran into my parents' room and found them cuddling.

'Quick, get up. I'm late for church,' I screeched.

They turned and looked at me as if I were an intruder.

'Sweetheart, what are you doing up so early?'

'It's Sunday. I'm making my First Holy Communion.' *What's the matter with them? Why are they smiling?*

'Well, off you go. You're a big girl now. You can go to the church on your own.'

What? The most important day of my life and they were acting like it was just any other day.

I ran back to the bedroom. I put on my dress, brushed my hair, and arranged my veil. White socks, white shoes, white gloves – check. I raced out the door.

I sprinted down Flemington Road and turned

right at Dryburgh Street. The hill was a challenge in the heat, but I kept up a fast pace, arriving at the church in a lather. Inside the large door, I saw a grim nun standing in the shadows; she sensed rather than saw me. Her face scrunched up in a scowl and she shook her head as she approached me.

With a bony hand digging into my shoulder – *ouch* – she marched me down to the front pews. The other girls shuffled along until space was made for me. A few people were 'tsk-tsking'.

Relieved to be in time to receive communion, I lined up with the other girls when the usher-nun got to our pew. I felt so holy taking the host – 'the body of Christ' – gently on my tongue. I was now a fully-fledged Catholic.

After mass, I went outside to ask the grim nun for my prayer book and rosary beads.

'You don't deserve to have them, you disrespectful child. How dare you be late for mass?'

I was mortified. Didn't she know what an effort I'd made to get there? Through my tears, I saw my parents walking towards me.

'Mummy, Daddy.' I sniffled as I ran into their outstretched arms.

'What's wrong, sweetheart?' My mother frowned.

'I'm being punished 'cause I was late. This nun won't give me my prayer book and rosary beads.'

'We'll see about that.' My mother turned to the nun, raised herself to her full height, leaned forward, and stared right into her eyes. The nun hurried off.

She came back with a prayer book and rosary beads in her hands.

You don't mess with the lioness, as Dad would say.

The Bigger They Are…

'Can we go play in the park, sir?' Franklyn implored our father.

Dad gave us permission after we'd promised to be home in time for dinner.

We took off across busy Flemington Road. A couple of friends joined us and we headed towards the thick forest, which divided the park from 'Camp Hell'. We didn't dare go through the forest in case we ran into the 'ruffians' who lived there in shacks.

Franklyn played Cowboys and Indians with his friends. I wandered off to look for field daisies. After a while, I came to a clear patch deep in the forest. When I looked up, I saw a mob of grubby kids moving towards me. I jumped up and ran away. One of my shoes came off, but I kept running until I reached my brother's gang.

'Franklyn! Franklyn! Help! I'm being chased by the ruffians.'

'Come over here, sis. Where's your other shoe?

'I lost it in the forest.'

'Geez, you'll cop it if we go home without it.'

My fearless brother took me by the hand and dragged me towards the forest.

'Uh-uh, I'm not going in there.' I pulled back.

Franklyn rallied the other boys in his John Wayne voice. 'Come on, guys, I need a posse.'

The sun was going down and it was getting spooky as we moved deeper into the forest. In a flash, we were surrounded by ruffians jumping out of the shrubbery.

'Have you got any money? How about lollies?' their leader said, grabbing at our pockets.

Who were these kids?

'Here, take my gun and leave us alone,' my brother said, handing over his favourite Christmas toy.

The head ruffian grabbed it and left, with the others looking over his shoulder at their booty.

'Come on, sis. We better get home.' Franklyn put his arm around my shoulder.

When we went inside the back gate, my parents were laughing with the Maltese guys. I could see red patches on my dad's body through his nylon shirt.

'What happened, Daddy? Why is your blood bleeding?' I ran to him and gave him a hug.

'It's okay, sweetheart. It's mercurochrome.'

'Uh?'

'Your father just beat up Gianni,' Joey said.

'Yeah. That dog scratched your dad. He had to go to hospital for treatment in case he got rabies.' Andy snickered.

'He beat Gianni to a pulp.' Charlie grinned.

'Oooh ... What happened, Daddy?' I said.

It turned out that Gianni, the landlord, had

grabbed my mother by the arm and thrown her out of the back laundry. Mum wasn't supposed to use it because it belonged to the boarder living in the bungalow. She ran to Dad in tears and showed him the red marks on her arm. He went ballistic.

Although Gianni was twice his size, my dad had been an unarmed combat instructor in the army. He grabbed Gianni's head under his arm and kept punching him in the face. Gianni had clawed at Dad because he couldn't breathe – that's how Dad ended up with all the scratches.

The good news was we didn't get into trouble for being late and losing my shoe. The bad news was we had to move digs. Again!

WEDDING COURT

The Big Move

My dad said, 'God moves in mysterious ways,' and I believe it. First, Julie wet herself in class, losing her so-called 'angel' status. Then the rickety old nun got 'put out to pasture'. *Good riddance!* I – the girl with brown hair and brown eyes – got to be the fairy queen in the Grade Two school concert (despite wagging ballet school). And just when we were going to end up on the street, we got offered a house in a new development. No cousins, no horrible landlords, no more moving, and I was getting my own bedroom. I wouldn't have to share with Franklyn. *Yay!*

I imagined it was the most beautiful house – it was in Wedding Court – and I would meet Prince

Charming there when I grew up.

Now that we were getting a place of our own, Mum was happy to stay in Australia. She gave the money she'd saved to Dad and he went to an auction and bought furniture.

The big day came. Joey and Andy offered to drive us to our new digs.

'Come on, CC, in you get.' Dad, using my new nickname, bundled me into the back seat of Joey's car. Franklyn, Lenny, and Mum were in Andy's car.

We drove forever until we got to a cluster of houses that were 'out in the sticks', as my mother said. Ours was the last one in the development; beyond our fence, flat empty land stretched to the horizon. The only things growing were tall purple thistles. Millions of them.

When we drove into the court, I could see there were no footpaths. Our house didn't have a front fence or a driveway either – just mud.

Dad carried me to the concrete house, opened the front door, then went back for Franklyn. Mum followed with Lenny in her arms. Joey and Andy brought in our suitcases.

The front door opened into the loungeroom that Dad had furnished with a couch and two chairs. The suite, upholstered in a faded tapestry material, had polished-wood arms. A lime-green padded 'dish' chair on spindly wooden legs sat in the corner, and a circular glass coffee table was placed on a Persian rug in the centre of the room.

My dad showed me into my bedroom, which stuck out from the front of the house. I rushed in and saw my parents' old bedroom furniture. Dad had painted it pale pink, decorated with a deeper pink diamond motif. It looked like a fairy princess's room.

The boys' bedroom had two single bookend beds and a chest of drawers. *Boring*.

Dad had furnished the master bedroom with a suite made of walnut, which included a huge oval-mirrored dressing table. I stood on its platform drawer and could see all of me!

In the kitchen, the table and chairs were a bit worse for wear, Mum said, but she looked pleased that her hard-earned money had stretched so far. She put on the kettle to make tea for the helpers.

'Well, what do you think, children?' Dad looked pleased with himself.

'It's really big. I love my bedroom furniture. Thank you, Daddy.' I hugged his legs.

'Where are all the other kids? Can I go out and play?' Franklyn couldn't have cared less about Dad's achievement.

Typical!

Lenny said nothing. Even though he was three years old, he didn't talk. He wasn't dumb, just pensive, Dad said.

Mum put the *pastizzi* in the oven. Twenty minutes later we were burning the roofs of our mouths with the piping hot ricotta oozing out of the flaky pastry.

After we'd eaten, Mum said, 'Come on, children.

Let's get your pyjamas on. You've had a big day and we have to get up early for church tomorrow.

I ran to my bedroom and got myself ready for bed. I was about to snuggle under the covers when I heard Dad calling out from the loungeroom.

'Come in here, children, and we'll say the Rosary. Remember, the family that prays together, stays together.'

Geez Louise! I could almost hear my mother thinking.

Religious Instruction

We had to walk forever to get to the church. Dad piggybacked me because my legs were wobbly from missing breakfast. That's what we had to do before taking Holy Communion.

I had on my best dress, my white bonnet, and gloves. Franklyn wore a suit, just like Dad. My mum looked elegant in her new floral dress and jacket. The tiny church was packed with parishioners, who looked as though they'd just come in their weekday clothes.

Didn't they realise they were entering the house of God?

After mass, we hung around outside, waiting to meet the priest. His name was Father Flannagan. My dad had to shield his eyes against the sun to look up at him.

'Welcome to the parish.'

'Bless me, Father.' Dad bowed his head.

Mum rolled her eyes and looked around to see if she could find some Maltese people.

'I'd like to start the children at Catholic school tomorrow,' Dad told the priest.

'We don't have a school here yet. They will need to enrol in the Glenroy parish.'

Even though there was a perfectly good state school five minutes up the street, the next day we traipsed along the road to Widford Street and caught the bus to Glenroy. We found the Mother Superior's office and Mum knocked on the door. It took forever for her to answer.

'Your children don't live in this parish. We can't accept them.' Mother Superior was curt.

'Seriously?' Mum's face was getting red. She took a deep breath, then exhaled. 'Well, thank God for that. I wouldn't want my children to go to a school where they'd feel like outsiders.' She grabbed our hands and threw the nun a word of advice. 'Maybe you should communicate more clearly with Father Flannagan. He seems to think they could be enrolled here.'

'Oh, well, if the Father said –'

Mum glared at the now frantic nun. 'Not going to happen. Try explaining that to the Father. Have a nice day.'

'Come on, children. Let's go get a treat at the shops, then we'll catch the bus home. Don't forget to tell your father what the Mother Superior said: you couldn't be enrolled. Okay?'

Is the Pope Catholic?

What a State

The next day, Mum took us to the state school. The headmistress walked me to the classroom and I was shown to a desk by my teacher.

'Welcome Cecile to our class, children.' The teacher looked and spoke like Colonel Pickering from *My Fair Lady*.

It was a vastly different experience to my first day at St Michael's. My desk-mate's name was June; she was from Ireland. She had blond hair and blue eyes but didn't act as if the sun shone out of her. And no one pointed out that she was an angel.

The morning passed quickly. I was feeling happy until I couldn't find my way home for lunch. I stood crying.

A teacher came up to me in the schoolyard.

'What's wrong, sweetie?'

'I'm lost. The aliens took my street away. All the houses are different.'

'It's okay. You were let out on the other side of the school. Here, take my hand. I'll show you your street.'

We walked to the end of the building and around the other side. There was my street. *Phew, what a relief!* I ran home as fast as I could.

Mum was waiting for me at the door.

'What took you so long? We were just about to send a posse.'

'Oh, Mummy, Mummy, I got lost. I can't go back to school today. I feel faint. I have to lie down.'

Mum rolled her eyes. 'What a drama, Sarah Bernhardt.' She always called me that when I got flustered. 'Come on. See what I made for lunch – bird's nests!'

I stopped crying and followed her into the kitchen. Franklyn was tucking into a plate of what looked like an artist's impression of a bird's nest – if you had a good imagination.

'I toasted the bread, piled on canned spaghetti, cracked an egg on top, and put it in the oven. Isn't it lovely?'

'Yes, Mummy.' I humoured her. Not that she wasn't a great cook, but sometimes she went off the deep end with her creations. It looked okay, but I wasn't hungry. After all, I'd just had an emotional breakdown.

'Franklyn, take your sister's hand and walk her to school. At home-time, collect her from her classroom and walk her home. Okay, Sarah, off you go.'

Meet the Neighbours

There was one other house in the court, opposite ours, which was vacant. About a month later, the Moores moved in. Mum went over to introduce herself and I tagged along. The door was opened by a woman with a deeply lined scowling face and a cigarette in her hand.

'Whaddayouseswant?'

Somehow, my mother was able to translate the one-word sentence.

'Hello, my name's Josephine. Call me Josie or Jo, if you like. This is my daughter Cecile.'

The woman stared down at me and sniffed. She took a drag of her cigarette and looked Mum up and down.

'I brought you a cake to welcome you to the neighbourhood.' Unfazed, Mum held out her famous chocolate cake. 'Thought it would be nice to have a cup of tea and get acquainted.'

'I don't do afternoon tea. I keep to meself. And I don't eat cake.'

'Well, I noticed you have a couple of kids. Maybe *they'd* like some cake.'

Mrs Moore was speechless for a while, then reached out and took the cake.

'Thank you.' She closed the door.

You've got to hand it to my mother, she had a heart of solid gold. And nerves of steel, to boot!

Some weeks later, we discovered that apart from Mr and Mrs Moore, there was Kevin, Keith, Lorraine, and the baby, David. Franklyn and I were playing ball in the court when one of the boys came over to us.

'Give us a throw.'

It wasn't a request.

Franklyn threw him the ball and the boy scurried away with it. We ran inside to tell Mum. Over to the Moores' we marched, and Mum knocked on the door.

'Your son forgot to return a ball to my kids. I've come to get it.'

What a diplomat!

'Kevin!' Mrs Moore shouted. 'Get out here.'

Kevin slouched towards the door, his eyes fixed on his plastic sandals.

As quick as a flash, Mrs Moore landed a slap to the side of his face.

'Give us that ball.' She handed the ball back to Franklyn and closed the door.

We stood there dumbfounded.

Later that afternoon, there was a knock at our door. It was Mrs Moore, surrounded by a brood of kids.

'Me name's Mary and me husband's Cliff. These are me kids.' She introduced them one by one. 'They know if they go causin' ya any trouble, they'll get a thumpin' from me.'

Without a by-your-leave, she turned around and walked away.

Life in the Sticks

We were settled in at school, there was a truce with the Moores, and finally we got footpaths and fences.

A semi-detached duplex was being built at the end of the court. I watched the tilers from my bedroom window, as I sat in the lime-green chair, bundled up with a blanket against the cold. Although we had a briquette heater, it was only lit at night when Dad came home.

I'd stayed home from school with tonsillitis and

Mum was making me chicken broth – her 'cure-all' remedy.

'Okay, come and get it,' she called to me.

I waved goodbye to the tilers and staggered into the kitchen.

'I-ma,' my mother said, rolling her eyes. It means 'What a pain' in Maltese.

She was telling me that my 'sick' act was a bit over the top.

Honestly, what did a child have to do to get some sympathy?

'Tomorrow, if you're feeling better, we could go to Mr Black's. I've seen he has new dresses in stock.'

My ears pricked up. Mr Black's was the only ladieswear shop in Olsen Place. Although he had two grown-up daughters, he acted as if I was his favourite child. Whenever I went to his shop, his face lit up and he greeted me with 'Hello, my princess'. Mum liked me to tag along because he always gave her a discount when she brought me in.

Back in my bedroom, I saw the bread van pull up in the court. Bread was home-delivered three times a week, fresh out of the oven. Mum went out, returning with two loaves, still warm. She cut us each a slice, smothering them with butter. *Yum!*

I loved spending time with Mum – just the two of us.

The smell of bread had woken Lenny. He tottered into the kitchen with his hand out and Mum gave him the slice she'd buttered for me.

On Fridays, the cake man drove over from Fawkner. It was the suburb whose lights we could see on the horizon at the end of the meadows. My favourite was chocolate slab cake. It wasn't a patch on Mum's devil's food chocolate cake, but in 'pay week' we always got 'bought' cake. It was more a treat for Mum than for us.

Our milk was delivered to the doorstep in bottles, the yellow cream sitting on the top of the white milk. Franklyn drank a whole bottle every day. I don't know how he did it. I still couldn't stand the stuff unless it was in a flavoured milkshake.

There were a whole bunch of other door-to-door salesmen. My mother felt sorry for them and ordered lots of stuff we didn't need. Dad told her to cancel the orders, but she didn't have the heart. When the orders arrived, she sent me to the door.

'Sorry, my mum's sick. She asked me to tell you we don't need the stuff she ordered.'

The salesmen left with hang-dog expressions. I felt awful.

Before long, Mum had amassed a clan of Maltese women. Once a month they came over for *bigilla* – a dish made with broad beans, garlic, oil, and parsley. Although it looked unappetising to me, they demolished it in minutes.

Mum's friends included Maria and Violet. Maria was a seamstress. Violet was a funny-looking person with Coke-bottle glasses, yet her kids all looked like angels.

The Wards were our new neighbours in the duplex next door. Mrs Ward was all twisted from having polio. My mother said she was a *miskina* – poor thing. She was on welfare because her husband was in a mental asylum for the criminally insane; he tried to murder her – *true story!* Her daughter kept to herself and the only time I heard a peep from her son was when he came to our door after school asking if he could watch 'TB'. He meant television; he was a bit slow.

We were the only people in the neighbourhood with a TV. Most afternoons, our loungeroom filled up with kids sitting on the carpet. They had to leave before Dad arrived. Mum said it was because he needed to relax after work, but he didn't know she let them come over.

The neighbourhood grew. We settled into our new place and felt part of a community. We didn't live in each other's pockets – as Mrs Moore would say – but we had each other's back. I felt safe walking down the street and I was happy at school where we were all Australians – like kangaroos – and the colour of our hair and eyes didn't matter.

Three

An Era

ALL ABOUT FAMILY

The Sergeant Major

It was Saturday morning and no school. *Yay!* I snuggled under the bed covers. That's when it started – band music!

'Rise and shine, children.'

The night before, Dad said he had a surprise for us. When we saw the record player we were thrilled. Little did we know he'd use it to blast us awake on Saturday morning.

'Paul! Turn that music down. Let them get some more sleep. They're your children, not your men.'

Thank goodness for my mother's common sense. Dad could be a bit over the top with his 'early bird catches the worm' philosophy.

My dad was one of those people who believed in

all things being regulated: waking times, meal times, television times, bed times. I wished he would go with the flow sometimes. I guess his army days instilled in him a discipline he couldn't shake off.

And then there was his commitment to religion. I believed in God and the Holy Mother Church, but my dad took it to a whole new level.

'Come on, Franklyn. Come on, CC. Let's go to confession so we can receive Holy Communion tomorrow.'

I had to make up sins when I got into the confessional. 'Bless me, Father, for I have sinned. I wished my dad's record player would break down.'

Franklyn, on the other hand, spent ages in the confessional. Dad joked about how the priest came out afterwards wiping the sweat from his brow.

I'm sure the congregation believed my brother was a hardened sinner. I supposed he was just better than me at making up transgressions. After all he was only twelve and a half years old.

'Waste not, want not,' Dad said when he recycled junk from the tip, much to my mother's dismay. He didn't think you should pay for something when you could get it for free.

One Saturday morning, Dad and Franklyn finished building an aviary for my brother's pigeon, aptly named 'Pidge'.

'Now, son, we need something to spread on the ground. Come on, let's get some sawdust from the butcher.'

Dad was dressed in overalls and a multi-striped leather beanie, which I suspected it was someone's cast-off. About half an hour later, they returned with a barrow-load of sawdust. Mum and I went out to greet them.

'Can you believe it, Jo?' That's what Dad called Mum sometimes. 'We walked into the shop as they were about to close, and the butcher waved his arms in the air and said, "No meat, no meat!" He nearly dropped dead when I said, "My good man, I haven't come for meat, I've come for sawdust".'

Dad had a refined English accent, which belied his olive complexion and dark brown wavy hair. In those days, if you didn't have blond hair and blue eyes it was presumed – by the morons in society – that you were illiterate.

If only the butcher could see Dad on a workday. He dressed impeccably in a navy double-breasted jacket with silver buttons, a crisp white shirt with a smart tie, and a pair of Fletcher Jones taupe slacks. On Sundays, he wore his best suit to church.

Dad worked at the Government Aircraft Factories in the personnel department and he had his own secretary. He was fluent in English, Maltese, and Italian, enabling him to translate for the Lebanese and Italian factory workers.

When we'd been in the area for three years, the mayor recommended my father for the position of Justice of the Peace. Dad was devoted to the community he lived in and helped uneducated people by writing letters for them and advocating on their behalf. I believe I got my sense of justice, fairness, and community spirit from my father.

Something else I got from my dad was a thirst for knowledge. He brought home maths puzzle books for me and, when we were still in primary school, he purchased a set of encyclopaedias on 'the never-never plan', as my mother said. He was paying it off for years. I showed my appreciation by reading it after school and on weekends until I'd finished all ten volumes. Franklyn, on the other hand, preferred *Phantom* comics and referred to himself as 'Phantom – ghost who walks'.

Spare me!

Jo, Josie, Jessie – a Rose by Any Name

Every Saturday morning my mother cooked us pancakes. I smelled their delicious aroma wafting from the kitchen through the loungeroom to my bedroom. If I didn't get up early enough, Franklyn would be on his second round and I'd get what was left.

'Good morning, Mum. The pancakes smell yum.'

'Thanks, sweetheart. Take a plate and get some before you-know-who eats them all.'

I piled pancakes onto my plate and smothered them in golden syrup. When we lived in New York we could buy maple syrup, but not in Australia. The country was backward, my mum said.

'Remember to say grace,' Dad reminded us as he came in from the loungeroom.

Of course we would. Heaven knows what would happen to us if we forgot.

After breakfast, Mum took me aside and whispered, 'Do you want to come to Mr Black's shop after breakfast?'

Did I ever?

I loved shopping for clothes with Mum. We had to keep it secret because my mother used to put the purchases on her 'account' and pay them off without Dad knowing. She loved buying me nice outfits, never splurging on herself.

After Dad had gone out to the garage to tinker, we sneaked out. Franklyn had already taken off to play with his friends. Lenny was reading a book on his own – the kid was one out of the box.

Outside, we saw Mrs Moore standing at her front gate having a cigarette and staring into the distance. We caught her eye, and she nodded in our direction.

'Hello, Mary, how are you?'

Mum smiled and waved.

'Still alive.'

Mrs Moore's economy with words left me stunned. Maltese people were chatty; it was unheard of for them to stop at two words.

We walked hand-in-hand to the shops, five minutes away and an easy stroll now that we had concrete footpaths.

'Hello, my princess. Come and see what I have

for you today.' Mr Black laid out a lemon light-wool twinset and an identical pink one.

'They're lovely. I don't know which one I like best. What do you think, Mum? The lemon twinset will go with my new green tartan skirt, but I like the pink one too.'

'Why don't you have both?' Mr Black encouraged.

My mother had a penchant for dressing me in all things pink, but I saw she was torn. She turned to Mr Black. 'Can I put one on layby?'

'Take them both now. I know I can trust you to pay them off.'

'Don't tell your father.' Mum wagged her finger at me when we left the shop.

As if I would.

The next day was the fortnightly Sunday when the 'freeloaders' came over for afternoon tea. That's what my dad called them. They were Mum's sister Mary, her four sons, and one daughter. My mother's hospitality was famous, so our cousins were accompanied by their girlfriends, boyfriend, mothers thereof, and even their close friends. We had to push the furniture aside to 'accommodate the masses', as Dad would say.

On Saturday afternoon, my mother began preparing for the feast. Dad harrumphed around the house, mumbling, 'Eating me out of house and home … Freeloaders!'

'Scrooge,' Mum said half under her breath, as she prepared the sausage rolls. The other savouries

– devils-on-horseback, club sandwiches, hollowed baguettes filled with cream cheese and gherkin – were made after church to ensure they were fresh. She also baked cupcakes and chocolate cake. The following day, she would transform them with cream into butterfly cakes, and with cream-cheese icing into Devil's food chocolate cake. Maltese trifle took the longest; the vanilla custard, fruit-in-jelly, and chocolate custard each had to set before the next layer was added. The date and walnut slices were delegated to me. I dusted them with icing sugar before serving the next day.

After church on Sunday, the table was piled high with goodies, then the 'rellos' arrived and devoured the food within ten minutes. It was like a plague of locusts stripping a field of corn, as Dad would say. Yet, if it wasn't for Auntie Mary giving us pocket-money, we wouldn't have had any money of our own, because my dad was a bit of a 'tight arse'.

On weekdays, before we woke to get ready for school, two women dropped off their young kids for my mother to mind while they worked in their factory jobs. The Maltese woman, Mrs Grixti, had two pre-schoolers: a boy and a girl. The Australian woman had two girls: one was in bubs grade and the other in Grade One. We took them to school with us, and their mum, Mrs Spears, picked them up when she finished work.

After the mothers left, Mum put the Maltese kids in the bath, because she saw a rim of dirt under their jumper sleeves. Their 'lunch' was buttered bread; my mother added cheese, ham, and salad.

'You should be charging extra, Mum.' I shook my head.

'I can't leave the kids dirty and hungry, can I? Their mother can't afford to pay more. She's struggling as it is.'

I suspected she wasn't paying Mum the going rate, but what could I say?

By contrast, Mrs Spears's daughters were clean and well-kempt, and their sandwiches were packed with filling. Her husband was an unemployed alcoholic, so she supported the whole family.

Go figure.

After school, I liked to change my clothes for something less plain.

'Mum, where is my gypsy dress? You know, the one with the lilac and pink diamond pattern and puffed sleeves?'

'Well, sweetheart,' – *hear it comes again* – 'you know that little girl who lives in Freda Street? Her father's been out of work for a long time and she doesn't have anything nice to wear. You have plenty of clothes. You just got the new twinsets and I thought you wouldn't mind if I gave her one of your dresses.'

A flashback of relinquishing my Cairo handbag to my Maltese cousin Natalie reminded me of my mother's tendency to give away my cherished belongings. I knew it was because of her kind heart, but I wished she'd given me a heads-up of her good intentions. It was my favourite dress, *for heaven's sake*.

There was a knock at the door.

'Mu-um! The Sri Lankan woman is here.'

My mother was always lending money to people. Sometimes they paid her back – this lady brought us a curry. *Bad news*. Mum asked for the recipe, then cooked it for us once a week. It was so spicy, my mouth burned for days afterwards. Not to mention …

My mother's kindness knew no bounds. When she volunteered to sell raffle tickets to raise money for our school, she asked my friend's mother to buy one.

'I can't even afford milk for the kids. My husband's been on strike for months, so we don't have a wage coming in.' The woman groaned, then drew on her cigarette.

'That's all right, I'll buy you a ticket.' My mother whipped out her purse without hesitation.

Blow me down if she didn't win the food hamper. The usually stiff-upper-lipped British woman cried when my mother delivered it. Her daughter told me later her mum thought my mother was an angel. I guess she was.

Brotherly Love

'Hey, sis, can I cut a piece of leather from your school satchel?'

'What for?' I reeled back, clutching the treasured bag to my chest.

'I need it for my ging.' Franklyn had made a slingshot after watching *Huckleberry Finn* on TV.

'What are you going to use it for?'

'Nothing.'

When Franklyn said 'nothing', you knew he was up to no good.

'Promise you're not going to hurt anything with it.'

'Promise.'

Liar.

His friend Goog let the cat out of the bag, so to speak, when he came over after school.

'Hey, Phantom, let's go to that old building on Camp Road and get some of those pesky sparrows.'

Goog was one of Franklyn's gang at high school. He hung around our place after school and on the weekends, getting up to all kinds of skulduggery with my brother. One day I saw them crawling through the trapdoor leading under our house. Franklyn noticed me watching them and beckoned me over.

'You can come with us if you don't tell Mum and Dad.'

I was curious; what *did* boys get up to on their adventures? I crawled in after them and we lay side by side on the cool damp ground, our noses a few centimetres from the floorboards.

Goog took out a packet of cigarettes and offered me one.

'Yuck. No thanks.'

He passed one to Franklyn and they lit up. They'd obviously done this before because neither of them coughed. Whereas I felt like I was choking in the confined space.

So, this was how boys passed the time. *Boring!*

'Hey, sis.' Franklyn frowned as he looked up from his homework books spread on the kitchen table.

What now?

'Will you do me a favour?' My *beloved* brother was all sweetness.

'Depends.'

'I can't do my English assignment and the teacher said she'll fail me if it's not handed in by next Monday. Dad will kill me if I fail.'

Good riddance.

I'd become wary of my brother's requests. It seemed like he always came out ahead from these exchanges.

'What's in it for me?'

'Do ya wanna come fishing with me and Goog on Saturday? We're going to ride our bikes down to Greenvale.'

I'd never been fishing and I'd yet to try out Franklyn's hand-me-down two-wheeler outside the court. Back in third grade, Billy Watts had taught me how to ride. He was sweet on me, but the friendship ended when he 'came the raw prawn', making a move on me in his cubby house.

'Okay, but you have to pay me 40 cents too.'

'Deal.' Franklyn looked like the cat who got the canary.

To complete the assignment, I had to read *Great Expectations* from cover to cover. I was fascinated with the story, but in hindsight I should have asked for 60 cents to do the assignment.

Saturday morning, after waking up to the dreaded army-band music, we stuffed our lunch into a backpack and raced off on our bikes. I felt exhilarated as I freewheeled down the steep slopes, oblivious to the danger of having no brakes.

After an hour, we arrived at our destination. We left our bikes under a tree and walked across the sun-scorched field to the riverbank. The boys carried the fishing gear; I, their designated squaw, carried the backpack.

It was hot and we soon depleted our supply of drinks. The fish weren't biting, but *we* were getting peckish. When we opened our lunch wrappers, we found ants had beaten us to our sandwiches.

'No worries,' said Goog. 'They haven't eaten much.'

His sense of humour was lost on me. I was starving, but I wasn't risking eating ants.

Goog, half Pom, half Scot, was one of Franklyn's many schoolfriends who hung about our house. Other members of my brother's gang included Boris from the Ukraine; Brian, the red-headed Scot; and several other acolytes of various nationalities.

I never understood the 'pull' my brother had. Whatever it was, I think my mother's generosity, with cookies and milk, was a contributing factor.

Franklyn was always getting up to mischief, whereas Lenny was content to read books on his own or hang around with me. He sought out my company from the time he was a toddler.

After school, I'd find him waiting inside the door and he'd tug at my sleeve until I agreed to play with him. We used to walk around the loungeroom swinging one hand in front of us singing: 'Hey-dee, hey-dee-ho, the great big elephant is so slow.' I even taught him a dance to Tchaikovsky's *Nutcracker Suite*. He loved that.

It wasn't all play, though. Lenny craved knowledge and was captivated when I read him Greek mythology from one of the encyclopaedias. His curiosity made him a quick learner, and he'd mastered basic reading and writing before he started school.

There was eight years' age difference between my two brothers. Franklyn saw Lenny as the 'fall guy' for his practical jokes. *Not on my watch, brother dearest.* I protected him from our older brother's taunts and comforted him when Franklyn's rough play reduced him to tears.

THE WAY THINGS WERE

The Neighbourhood

Over the years, the housing development grew in all directions. In the court adjacent to the Wards – but on the flip side – the Dowds with their two kids shared a fence with us. They kept to themselves.

Mrs Dowd looked like a woodpecker. She had two woodpecker kids and a stork of a husband. In summer, we watched from our back porch as she hung out her washing, clad only in her underwear. My mother thought it was scandalous; she bundled us inside the house to protect our morals from being damaged.

The Collards, with their five kids, moved into the semi-detached house next to the Dowds. Three of the

Collard girls – Judy, Jenny, and Cathy – vied to be my playmate. Their older sister Deidre – God help her – fancied Franklyn. Almost every week, Mrs Collard sent the girls over to borrow sugar, milk, coffee, tea, and a variety of other foodstuffs from us. Mum lent her money too, which was never repaid. My mother once said the only thing she hadn't borrowed was my dad.

Shortly after the Collards moved in, Judy called to me from her corner of the fence. 'Wanna come over to my place and climb into the ceiling?'

I was game. Over the fence I went and followed Judy in. She dragged a ladder over to the manhole.

Who keeps a ladder inside?

When we'd climbed to the top and scrambled into the ceiling cavity, Judy pulled out a pack of cigarettes and a lighter.

'Wanna fag?'

'No thanks, I'm too young to smoke.' I was a year younger than her.

Judy, it turned out, was the female equivalent of Franklyn's friend Goog.

'Please yaself.'

Entranced, I marvelled at the way she blew smoke rings. She was eleven but smoked like a film star.

Behind us, in the next court along Ernest Street, a Dutch family moved in with a million kids. They had an above-ground pool and invited the neighbours' young kids in for a swim during the Christmas holidays. Full of glee, Lenny scrambled up the ladder that was permanently leant against our side of the shared fence.

Within ten minutes, my brother was standing at the back door sobbing his little heart out.

'What's the matter?' I rose from the kitchen table and gave him a hug.

'A big boy punched me.' He rubbed a reddening patch on his face.

Mum took off at great speed. Without a 'by your leave', she catapulted herself over the fence, her feet not once touching the rungs of the ladder.

There was a loud cry of surprise as my mother wacked the offending child. 'Now you know what it feels like to be hit by someone bigger,' I heard Mum say.

I could hear the other kids cheering her on. Apparently, he was the neighbourhood bully.

'I'm gonna tell my mum on you,' the boy wailed.

'Be my guest!'

Half an hour later, there was a knock on the door. I had a feeling of déjà vu, remembering Mrs Rolypoly from Brooklyn.

'Tell your mother I've come to see her about hitting my son.' The woman with a strong Northern English brogue stood with arms crossed, her nostrils flaring.

My mother came to the door, went outside, and walked her to the end of the driveway. Nonetheless, I could hear the woman hurling nasty comments at Mum. She finished her tirade with an attack on Mum's ethnic origins. 'Why don't you go back where you came from?'

Mum remained calm. 'Why don't *you* go back to England?'

There was a drawn-out silence. I was too far away to make out the rest of the conversation. Within minutes they were smiling; the feud was over. Turned out she'd heard about my mother's kind gesture to her friend, for whom Mum had bought the winning raffle ticket for a hamper. *Small world.*

The people who lived on the other side of the Collards had two huge daughters, Cheryl and Jill. Cheryl was grown up and had a job – she was a recluse. Jill, on the other hand, was outgoing and friendly. She wore dangly earrings and painted her nails bright pink. A devoted fan of Elvis Presley, she offered to take a bunch of the older kids from the neighbourhood to see his latest movie.

I was pleasantly surprised that Mum let me go with her. Jill was fifteen, hardly an adult.

We caught the train to Brighton and went to the Dendy. Jill kept us amused with stories about Elvis, and the time passed quickly on the long journey in the summer heat.

After the movie, she bought us ice-cream. We ate sitting on the beach, cooling down from the oppressiveness of the cinema.

When we got home after 11 pm, my mother was having conniptions. I guessed she hadn't counted on us being so late and was worried.

We weren't allowed to go out with Jill again.

Cecile Ravell

That's Entertainment

Each fortnight, after the 'rellos' had consumed Mum's Sunday feast, our cousins and their entourage took off, leaving Auntie Mary and her eldest son Charlie at our place. They were joined at the card table by Leonida and George Bugeja, Joe Buttigieg, and Father Lawrence, a Maltese priest.

The kitchen filled with the cigarette smoke of a bunch of people concentrating on their cards. The tension in the room was palpable; it was high stakes poker, with about five dollars in the kitty.

'Come and stand next to me for good luck.' Joe beckoned me over. He used to take me and Lenny to the soccer when George Cross FC was playing. I felt I had an obligation to be his lucky charm.

Auntie Mary acted like she was playing for sheep stations. For someone who was generous with giving away her money, she hated losing at cards. She would exclaim 'uff' when she was bluffed out of the game. The playing went late into the night, with Mum replenishing the players' energy with *pastizzi*, tea, and *biscotti*.

After a while I got bored and sneaked off to my bedroom to read a book, escaping to Anne Shirley's world of Green Gables.

One Saturday each month we were treated to a drive-in movie. My mother cooked hamburgers with exotic fillings. I had the job of wrapping and putting them in a picnic basket, along with a flask of coffee, soft drinks, and bags of chips and lollies.

'Now, don't expect to buy any food at the drive-in.' Dad shook his finger as we piled into the car.

'Cheapskate,' Mum said, half under her breath.

As we waited in line to pay our entrance fee, Dad told Franklyn to shrink himself down in the seat. When you had limited funds to spend on entertainment, you watched every penny. I couldn't help thinking: if Dad gave less to the church, we'd have tons more money to splurge on treats.

We finished our hamburgers, chips, and Coke during the opening ads; by the time it was interval, we were hungry again. Under the guise of taking us to the washroom, my mother bought us treats from the cafeteria.

'Don't tell your father.'

Yes, Mum, we know the drill.

Hooray, school holidays! We got to sleep-in, play all day, and go into the city.

Mum was dressed in her best clothes when she came out of the bedroom. 'Come on ... hurry up. We need to catch the early train so we can get into the city in time for lunch before the movies.'

What a treat! The city and the movies.

'Sweetheart, help Lenny get dressed.'

Franklyn was already out the door.

I loved trains. There were only two occasions when

I got to ride: when Mum took us to the city, and when Dad took me to Mrs Barski's house. I used to play with Mrs B's sausage dog Gretchen, while Dad undertook minor repairs to her apartment building in Ripponlea. She was as rich as, but only ever gave us liverwurst on stale bread for lunch.

I gazed longingly at the houses we passed on the train ride to the city. They were grand compared to our humble concrete one. I longed to live in a cream-brick house and dreamed of owning one when I grew up.

The 'red-rattler' pulled into Flinders Street Station and my older brother was first off.

'Franklyn, wait for your brother and sister,' said Mum.

Sure, like that was going to happen.

'Hold your brother's hand, Cecile, and help him get down.'

Lenny was so skinny I believed my mother was frightened he would slip between the train and the platform.

'Wait 'til I catch you,' Mum shouted as Franklyn ran towards the exit. He was grabbed by a station master who held onto him until she caught up to them. Mum gave Franklyn a clip around the ear.

'Now, stay close to me, you little imp, or you won't get any ice-cream when we go to the movies.'

Franklyn fell into line with us, the look on his face defiant.

We arrived at Myer and saved a table while Mum

queued to get our lunch. Food in Myer's café was much more up-market than Coles cafeteria, and more expensive. But this outing was our once-a-year treat and my mother made sure that it was the best time ever.

Love you, Mum.

After lunch, we browsed the ladies' clothing department. My mother didn't try on any clothes – she just liked to look.

We left Myer and walked to The Capitol Theatre in Swanston Street. The lights had already dimmed and an usher shone his torch down the richly carpeted aisle as he walked us to our seats in the front row.

Mum pointed up to the ceiling; covered in tiny lights, it looked like the night sky. *Cool.* It sure beat the Glenroy scout hall with its dusty wooden boards and the 'great unwashed' – as Dad called them – shouting and carrying on to such a degree I found it impossible to enjoy the movie. And don't get me started on the obligatory Jaffa-rolling down the aisle.

The crimson drapes parted as the film's introductory music played. The movie was *The Nutty Professor*, starring Jerry Lewis. When I 'wagged' ballet classes and went to the theatre in Errol Street, I saw him in movies with Dean Martin. I didn't expect this movie to be any good without his on-screen pal, but it was hilarious. When he sang 'That Old Black Magic' as Buddy Love – the sophisticated playboy – I was enthralled. I thought he looked *so* handsome.

Our day out ended, but we had a summer of holiday fun and adventure to look forward to.

Life's a Beach

Dad was a champion swimmer. When he was seven years old, his father lowered him on a rope, over a cliff in Malta, and told him to start stroking. He was so focused on getting his technique right, he didn't notice his father had dropped the rope.

Dad swam off the rocks every day during Malta's summer, but the beaches in Australia held no appeal for him. 'They're covered in sand,' he said.

Dur, Dad.

The situation worsened when we saw a movie about a human arm that was found in a grey nurse shark. That was it – the beach was out.

Fortunately for us, our cousins loved the beach. When we went to their place, on the second Sunday 'rello' rotation, Charlie took us to Geelong. We splashed around in the shallows, digging out pippies – small clams – with our toes. After collecting a bucketload, we took them into shore; Mum washed and served them to us raw, with a squeeze of lemon.

'You want *hobz bi zeit*?' My Auntie Mary handed me a piece of Maltese Vienna bread, smeared with olive oil and fresh tomato – food of the gods.

Franklyn had already wolfed down his second piece. It was all I could do to catch up.

'I'll help you eat that, sis,' he said, snatching it from my hand before running down the beach.

'Muuuum! Franklyn took my *hobz bi zeit.*'

'Franklyn! Come here, you little imp! Wait 'til we get home and I tell your father.'

Like anything's going to happen, Mum. Please!

'Here, have another piece.' Mum gave me a fresh slice.

Auntie Mary laughed at me. She didn't have Mum's sensitivity. Sometimes I wondered if they were truly sisters. But then, how did I end up with a brother like Franklyn?

It was getting late. Charlie bundled us into his EJ Holden and we started the long journey home. I was allowed to sit in the front seat because he wanted to avoid having me throw up, like I did on the way there.

Although the sun had gone down, the air was still sweltering. Cars were breaking down all over the place. While we waited for the traffic to move, we got out and walked around to escape the stifling air.

The bumper-to-bumper trip back to Altona took us two hours and, when Charlie pulled the car into the driveway, we saw Dad standing with his arms crossed, waiting for us.

'What took you so long? I have to work tomorrow. The kids are starting back at school. What were you thinking, keeping the kids out so late, Josephine?' That's what he called Mum when he was angry.

She had not been thinking at all – she was a 'go

with the flow' kind of person. Besides, it wasn't as if she had any control over the situation. Charlie was the driver and it wasn't his fault the traffic was a nightmare.

On the way home, as was his habit, Dad started saying the Rosary. I was out cold by the time I got halfway through the first Holy Mary!

THE GETTING OF WISDOM

Songs and Sinners

We played school ping-pong for the first two years after we moved to Wedding Court. The Education Department, in all its wisdom, kept re-zoning the borders, oblivious of how this impacted the lives of children in primary school. When I returned to my previous school, in fourth grade, I hoped that's where I was going to stay.

My friendship with June was re-established and I chose her to partner me in a song and dance number for the school concert.

I invited her to my house to go through the musical routine. She needed a lot of tutoring – unlike me, the experienced diva! We practised 'Pennies from Heaven' in my bedroom. Afterwards, I went through my jewellery box and offered June my pearls to wear for the performance.

'Are you thirsty? Would you like a soft-drink?' I said as I walked out of the room towards the kitchen.

I came back with two glasses of Coke and noticed June wearing a sheepish look. It wasn't until I opened the jewellery box again that I saw the 40 cents Franklyn had paid me to do his homework was missing.

Unfazed, I looked June in the eye. 'When I left the room there was 40 cents in my jewellery box. I'm going to take our empty glasses to the kitchen. Would you look for the money while I'm away?'

When I came back, the 40 cents had been returned. No use ending a friendship over a moment of weakness.

Villains and Heroes

On the first day of Grade Five, Mum made peanut-butter cookies and packed them in my lunchbox, which I left in the storage shelves outside our classroom. At playtime, the cookies had disappeared. I burst into tears. Our teacher, Miss Fitzgerald, came out of the classroom and saw my distress. She bent down, putting a soothing hand on my shoulder.

'What's the matter, dear?'

I choked back a sob. 'Someone took the cookies my mum made.'

'There, there. When recess is over, I'll find out who the culprit is. Go outside now and get some fresh air.'

Out in the play area, I saw one of the boys eating cookies out of my lunchbox. Without thinking, I ran at him and smacked him in the mouth.

'Would you like blood with those cookies, you thief?'

A group of boys gathered around and watched the offender, Rex, hand back my lunchbox.

'Wow.' One of the boys was roaring with laughter. 'You really can punch.' The amazed boy was Russell, the stocky half of the Scott twins, the other being skinny Peter.

'Whadayareckin, Pete? Is she fantastic, or what?'

I had scored an admirer.

'Say sorry, Rex, or else.' Russell brandished a fist at his friend. 'And if ya mess with her again, you'll answer to me.'

At lunchtime, Russell handed me some money. 'This is for you.'

'What for?'

''Cause you're the best sheila in the world.'

From that day forward, Russell followed me everywhere. Peter, the silent twin, tagged along.

No one stole my cookies again.

Friends and Aspirations

I had seated myself at the back of the classroom, diagonally opposite the teacher's desk. The door slid open next to me. A miniature man walked in, his trouser cuffs frayed from being trodden on by the heels of his shoes.

'Good morning, my name is Mr Giddings. Welcome to Grade Six.' Our new teacher smiled as he cast his eyes around the class.

I could barely see the top half of his body when he stood on the platform at the front of the room. He looked like a leprechaun, with his bulging eyes and scrunched-up face.

The door slid open again and a girl with a long dark-blond plait sneaked into the room. I beckoned her to take the vacant half of my desk.

Mr Giddings pretended not to notice her lateness. I liked him instantly.

'I'm going to give you a test now. The students with the highest marks will sit in the back seat, the next highest in the seat in front and so on. As your marks improve, you will move towards the back of the row.' Mr Giddings walked around the room handing out the test papers.

I got the highest mark in the class and retained my seat. The girl who'd plonked herself next to me, Beth, got the second highest mark by occasionally looking over my shoulder and copying my answers. I didn't mind. I was curious to get to know this girl who dared to turn up late on the first day of school.

Lunchtime came before we knew it and the girls in our row met outside. We sat on the grass, eating our lunch and getting to know each other. Beth was from England, Dawn was Australian, Sandra bussed in from

Beveridge with her brother, there was June who I'd known since fourth grade, and Annabella, the Russian.

After the break, Mr Giddings called us to his desk, one at a time, to ask if we had any concerns about our schoolwork. When my turn came, I noticed the index and middle fingers of his right hand were stained with nicotine. He had smokers' breath and it was all I could do to stop myself from gagging.

'It's clear from your test results that you won't have any issues, Cecile. I thought to be fair to your classmates, I should appear to be asking you the same questions that I'm going to ask them.'

How considerate.

For the entire year, I retained my position in the back seat. But one day, when I was away sick, Mr Giddings sprung a test. Beth's results dropped and she had to relinquish her position in the back seat. She was moved next to Dawn, who replaced me as her best friend. *Oh well.*

Despite being the shortest girl in the class – the Maltese used to be pigmies – I was selected for the basketball team. The coach was the fourth-grade teacher, Miss Harris. Although she was on the stocky side, she moved with agility on the court. After practising goal shooting with all the team, she chose me as goalie. Valerie Shipway was the attack wing. Beth said she was 'up herself'. Her turn of phrase cracked me up.

On the court, Valerie kept me out of the loop; she took all the goal shots herself, often missing. I complained to Miss Harris, who stepped in and held a competition at goal throwing. I won. From that day on, Valerie began openly insulting me every chance she got. I ignored her, but when she made nasty comments about my mother, I blew a fuse. I told the other girls in our row what she'd said about my mother's weight, and they started calling her 'Valerie Shit-way' until she stopped bullying me.

We won the pennant that year and Miss Harris took us to town for the day. We went to Captain Cook's cottage and had lunch in the nearby gardens. Afterwards we watched *My Fair Lady*. I thought Audrey Hepburn was the most beautiful woman I'd ever seen. I liked that she had brown hair, too.

After first term, we were joined by a newcomer from Finland. Her name was Ulla. Her hair was almost white, and she had the pinkest skin and clearest blue eyes that I'd ever seen. She sat next to Annabella and became part of our lunch group.

When a new community pool opened in the Autumn term, we discovered Ulla was a champion swimmer. The rest of the gang shivered at the edge of the outdoor pool, while Ulla gleefully swam laps like a bloody dolphin.

'Come on, girls. In you go,' said Miss Harris.

'No bloody way.' Beth was adamant.

'Miss, I've got my period.' Dawn used that excuse for every sports activity.

'I've got a cold,' Sandra declared.

I couldn't lie, so I jumped in. *Bloody hell!* It was freezing.

Thankfully, the pool was closed the next week due to a leak and not re-opened until summer.

There is a God.

In term three, Mr Giddings began interviewing us about our career aspirations. I knew what I wanted to be: a secretary. When I was in Grade Three, Dad's secretary invited us for afternoon tea on Christmas Day. She gave all the kids a present; mine was a tiny book – *Thumbelina* – which I cherished.

I liked everything about her: her manners, her clothes, her neat hair. She reminded me of Audrey Hepburn. I wanted to be like her and maybe become my dad's secretary one day.

Mr Giddings almost choked when I told him. He calmed himself down and said, 'You have the intelligence to set your sights higher, Cecile. Why don't you go down to the bubs class and assist the teacher? I think you might change your mind.'

I did.

At the end of the Grade Six year, I prepared to make my Confirmation. No going back from there – this was a solid commitment to the faith! I attended Catholic religious instruction classes every week and knew the catechism backwards. After church, I went along with Beth to the Church of England Sunday school classes. I got all the catechism answers right and cleaned up with a booty of lollies as a reward. What can I say? A throwback to my marble-playing days – once a hustler, always a hustler!

Franklyn's schoolfriend Brian was in a band and offered to play at my Confirmation party – *free*. At last, a ripple benefit for being Franklyn's sister.

As per usual, my mother prepared a humongous feast. The loungeroom was filled with the 'rellos', accompanied by their entourage. Beth arrived and said her mother told her not to eat any of our weird food – *her loss!*

The Maltese custom was to give the confirmees – *is that a word?* – money. Lots of it. Dad held it for me and said I should put it in the bank on Monday. *Good old thrifty Dad.*

The boys in the band stopped for a break and a snack. Out of the blue, the introverted Lenny said to Brian, 'Get back to work, what do you think you're being paid for?'

Franklyn grabbed Lenny by the scruff of the neck and marched him outside, once more regaining his hero status in my eyes.

I saw Brian's face had turned red and I wished the floor would open and swallow me up.

'I am so sorry. He's just a kid. Would you like to share my Communion money?'

'All I want is a kiss,' he said. 'That's sufficient payment for the pleasure of being in your company.'

How gallant.

He took my hand and brushed his lips against it.

My whole body tingled. I blushed and looked away.

My primary school life ended the way it had started – with a kiss. My childhood years were now behind me, but the magic would live in my mind and heart forever.

Acknowledgements

I am grateful for parents who had the courage and determination to travel half-way around the world in search of a better life for their family; for being imbued with the grit to overcome the negativity that was thrown at me by a culture that saw me as "less than"; and for the primary school teachers who inspired and encouraged me.

In polishing this story, I spent many days with my friend and "partner in crime", laughing, talking, and lunching, while we edited. Thanks, Magz Morgan, for your camaraderie and support and for your review of *Child Magical*.

Pennies from Heaven: from Pennies from Heaven, w Johnny Burke, melody Arthur Johnston. © 1 c. May 1, 1936; E unp. 123687; Select music publications, inc., New York. 14575

I have extensively searched for copyright ownership to no avail. I believe that my use falls within 'Fair Use' guidelines.

Cover image: Shutterstock

Cover design: newartworx.com.au

About the Author

Cecile Ravell is a creative memoir author and poet. She was born in 'Hell's Kitchen', in Midtown Manhattan, and spent her early childhood in Brooklyn, NYC. Her family returned to Malta when she was four years old, then immigrated to Melbourne, Australia, when she was five. She lives in a 'leafy' suburb of Melbourne.

She spends her time travelling the world and writing, and attributes her love of travelling to her early life. Her novellas include *Love on a Faultline* and *Dilemmas of a Middle-aged Madonna*. She has won first prize for her short-story 'The Drama of Dying', and for two flash-fiction stories 'On My Merits' and 'Not So Cocky Now'. Her collection of short stories and poetry will be published in *The Soul Bared*, and a selection can be previewed at https://ravellc.wixsite.com/ravell-the-writer/blog.

www.ingramcontent.com/pod-product-compliance
Lightning Source LLC
Chambersburg PA
CBHW021411290426
44108CB00010B/489